THE EVERYDAY LEADER

...using your past and present
...to improve your future

STUART KLEIN

Copyright © 2021 Stuart Klein

Published in 2021

Published for Stuart Klein by Verité CM Limited,
124 Sea Place, Worthing, West Sussex BN12 4BG
+44 (0) 1903 241975

email: enquiries@veritecm.com
Web: www.veritecm.com

The right of Stuart Klein to be identified as the Author of this Work has been asserted by him in accordance with the Copyright, Designs and Patents Act 1988.

All rights reserved. No part of this publication may be reproduced, stored in a retrieval system or transmitted, in any form or by any means, without the prior written permission of the publisher.

British Library Cataloguing in Publication Data
A record for this book is available from The British Library

ISBN: 978-1-914388-11-8

Printed in the UK

The everyday Leader...

I have had the privilege of working with Leaders at all levels, across a range of Nations and Sectors, for over thirty years.

I have always sought to facilitate Leadership understanding, knowledge and improvement, in a very practical manner. The aim of development is always to enable the Leader and their people to improve their contribution to their organisation and future.

I am so grateful for the work of many Leadership specialists who have committed their work and understanding, for the benefit of others. Some have been used and referenced in The Everyday Leader, with acknowledgements. Why re-invent the wheel?

My final point is that I have attempted to provide a practical and structured review process. Like any improvement it requires commitment and investment.

It will be worth it!!

Stuart Klein

In memory:

Eileen, who was my constant support and encourager, who made so much possible.

Forever grateful......

Make reflections on the area covered:

How am I doing with the above? Which relationships do I need to improve?

Identify a couple of people from your Seniors/Colleagues/Team. What will you do?

Month 1	Month 2	Month 3

Actions I must take:

(Where I need to improve..........)

1. _____ by _____ Yes

2. _____ by _____ Yes

3. _____ by _____ Yes

4. _____ by _____ Yes

5. _____ by _____ Yes

6. _____ by _____ Yes

Day 2

See with VISION!!

It's great to have a Vision in life - for a Leader its absolutely crucial!

Your Vision is derived from your passion.

This is what you 'sell' every day to your followers. No clear vision means you don't have anything to sell.

It's crucial that you know where you are going and how you are going to get there.

Effective Leaders see the bigger picture; where they are heading and what they need to do to arrive at their destination. A Vision should be captured in a single sentence. It's then easier to communicate and remember, particularly for followers.

A Leader without a vision is lost! They don't know the journey, so how can they expect followers to be enthusiastic about it. Once the Vision is known, the journey can be planned. (That's Strategy!)

Imagine you are on a plane waiting for take-off and the Captain's voice comes over the speaker,

> 'Good morning ladies and gentlemen. Today we will take off soon and then we will fly south. We'll cruise at about 33,000 feet. When we have about a quarter of tank of fuel left, we'll look for somewhere to land'

How are you feeling? Very nervous I would think!

What you would like to hear is,

> 'Good morning ladies and gentlemen. We will be taking off when our slot is confirmed, in the next 5 minutes. We'll be flying south and then over France. We'll be cruising at 33,000 feet and our estimated time of arrival is 11.30am local time. The weather there at the moment is sunny and 21 degrees. I'll update you nearer the end of our journey.'

Look the different approach of these two Leaders. The first Leader does not have a destination, no journey plan and no clear details. The Team are left wondering 'What's it all about?'
The second has instilled real confidence for those who are on the journey.

A clear Vision is crucial and will:

1. Motivate and inspire yourself and others
2. Identify priorities
3. Avoid the 'day-today' drudgery

ACTION:

> *Now think about your own Leadership.*
>
> **Do you have a clear Vision?**
>
> **Write it out in a sentence**
>
> **How are you selling the vision to your followers?**

Make reflections on the area covered:

Develop your own Vision Statement!

My Vision statement:

In _____ years time, I will:

Now what do you need to do to 'sell' your Vision to others?

Commit yourself to actions

Month 1	Month 2	Month 3

1. _____ by _____ Yes

2. _____ by _____ Yes

3. _____ by _____ Yes

4. _____ by _____ Yes

5. _____ by _____ Yes

6. _____ by _____ Yes

The everyday Leader......

Introduction

Welcome to this self review, aimed at you, the Leader. One thing that stops real improvement is our inability to stand back and review how we are doing. Business can be 'busy-ness'. We are locked into the ever demanding here and now. It takes real effort to step back and examine performance. 'Stepping back', on a regular basis, adds real value to our Leadership performance, our lives and in turn, our organisations.

Here's a great opportunity for you!

I've been stepping back on a daily basis for a number of years. The personal benefits for me and those around me, I believe, have been enormous. Having a structured approach is crucial.

Effective learning requires repetition. This Manual requires you to repeat each day in each of the next three months, to aid retention and increase benefits. It's a strange thing, but you will possibly discover something different from the same information, reviewed at different times.

The Process

Included in this Leader's Manual is **a daily, structured and yet practical approach**, all arranged in bite-sized chunks. The contents are areas that are commonly associated with effective Leadership. Many people exercise on a daily basis – why not do Leadership exercises?

How do you measure up? Now is the time to find out!!

Process:

1. Read through and study each daily topic.

2. As you work through the material, **make notes** about its application to you, your performance and your Team/Individuals.
   This will require you to consider what is actually happening in the areas of your Leadership

3. Determinedly complete the **ACTION,** relating to each page (No short cuts!)
   Each day has a facing page to help you do this.
   Complete your notes in the relevant month. (eg Month 1; Month 2; Month 3)

4. Finally, choose the time of day that suits you and stick to it. Don't make excuses

REMEMBER:

You receive a return on the investment you put in. There is little doubt in my mind that you will improve your Leadership effectiveness by investing regularly, by:

> **reflecting** on your performance/experiences
> > **identifying** changes required
> > > **implementing** identified improvements
> > > > **re-evaluating/measuring** the improvements

The everyday Leader....... *your record* (Date the column when covered, over Month 1,2 3)

Day 1	Win a heart before you ask for a hand			
Day 2	See with VISION!!			
Day 3	Where's your Leadership authority?			
Day 4	The first four minutes….			
Day 5	What motivates…			
Day 6	Changing your people....			
Day 7	A Balanced Leader....			
Day 8	The power of words...			
Day 9	Spend the 80% on the 20%			
Day 10	Everything rises or falls on Leadership			
Day 11	Go the 'extra mile'			
Day 12	The Customer Thing			
Day 13	Manage yourself...			
Day 14	The Leader v The Manager			
Day 15	Body Language says it all....			
Day 16	Who will you influence today?			
Day 17	Timing is crucial....			
Day 18	A Leader's courage			
Day 19	Coach for success			
Day 20	Personal attitude – how important!!			
Day 21	Communicating to win			
Day 22	Balance your life…			
Day 23	Three Levels of Leadership			
Day 24	The power of Teams and Individuals!!			
Day 25	Credibility is a must…			
Day 26	'Stay ahead of the game'			
Day 27	The loneliness of a Leader…			
Day 28	Servant Leadership!!			
Day 29	Different people – different support			
Day 30	The power of potential – if it's used...			
Day 31	The Klein Leadership Profile			

Day 1

'Win a heart, before you ask for a hand'

Leaders at all levels, in any organisation, must engage others and lever out of them, excellent standards of work and effort. **'Winning a heart'** is the first step in this process.

People buy into people. You can have everything as a Leader, but if you can't get people to **'buy' into you,** you are doomed to failure, or if you are fortunate, only average performance.

Effective Leaders get commitment from all those around them and from every level, including their Seniors. Remember, managing upwards is as crucial as managing your Team.

How do you build your relationships?

If you are an outgoing personality, it helps. Introverts must be prepared to 'push' themselves to interact. Our behaviour is also crucial. Our words are whispering to others, but our actions are shouting. People watch us like hawks when we are Leaders. Then they mirror our behaviour.

Remember also, that over half of the message we deliver, is via our gestures and body language. You can say the greatest things, but it must all be reinforced by what you do and how you behave. This integrity builds respect and trust, which are the bedrock of all good relationships

One other vital area in building this rapport, is honouring our word and commitment to others. Not fulfilling our promise pulls relationships down. Doing what we promise, deposits greatly into our 'goodwill' bank, with others.

I meet Leaders who don't think that relationships are important. They think the **Task** is the most important thing. 'Everything is ok, as long we get the job done!' This couldn't be further from the truth! It's **people** who do the work and if they are not treated with value, it will affect their commitment to the Task and more importantly, the Leader.

ACTION:

Here are five golden Rules for building great relationships, at work and everywhere else too.

Check your behaviour:

	Yes	No
1. I welcome others when they approach me.	☐	☐
2. I listen to what people are saying and show by my gestures, that I am listening	☐	☐
3. I keep my word and honour commitments to all the people around me	☐	☐
4. I go out of my way to communicate with others	☐	☐
5. Where praise is due, I give it!	☐	☐

Any areas marked 'No' are areas where you could be doing better!

Action:

> **Go on today – 'Win a heart', then ask for the 'hand'.**
>
> **Commitment from others will be forthcoming.**

Day 3

Where's your Leadership authority?

Every Leader needs authority. Without it, they cease to be a Leader. Authority elevates the Leader above the Team Members.

Authority is:
> 'The power to determine, control or command'

It is a right however, that has to be earned.

Where does **AUTHORITY** come from? Three areas:

1. Position — This occurs when the organisation 'officially' appoints one of its members and confers a title on them. eg. Supervisor, Manager, Director, etc..
It is crucial that any appointment is made public and communicated to everyone. If people don't know that an Individual has Leadership authority, why should they listen to them and respond positively?

2. Experience/ Knowledge — Team members who have experience and knowledge are sought after by others. People ask for their opinion. A Leader who has come 'through the ranks' has developed experience and this can be used to great effect in leading the team. Knowledge/experience stops Team Members from 'pulling the wool' over the Leader's eyes. The Team also respects experience/ knowledge. Without knowledge and experience, the Leader has to rely heavily on the Team and get up the learning curve 'as quickly as possible'.

3. Personality/ Behaviour — The great, but I think, meaningless, debate over the years, has been, 'Are Leaders born or made?' Futile, really, as it is crucial for **all** Leaders to have great people skills. Some personalities find this easier than others. However, all skills can be learned and developed by anyone – including you and I.
Essentially, **Leadership is majorly about people**, not process.
So, effective Leaders, continually work hard on their people skills – listening, watching their Body Language, knowing how to motivate the range of very different Team members.

Effective Leaders perform well in all these three areas.

What happens if Leaders are only running off:

1. Position — People only do 'just enough' to ensure they 'don't get punished'.
They will not go the extra mile for the Leader.

2. Experience/ Knowledge — *Better!* The Leader has the position *and* the required knowledge/experience, so people will seek them out for this, though there is still a need for the Leader to project themselves.

3. Personality — *Even Better*, if the Leader is **running off all three!**
Effective Leaders have heightened people skills – the ability to influence and get others to follow.

ACTION:

What are you running off?

Position ☐   Knowledge/Experience ☐   Personality ☐

Make reflections on the area covered:

How am I doing with the above?   What will I do and when?

Do I need to improve my 'people skills?' What will I do? When?

Month 1	Month 2	Month 3

Actions I must take:

(Where I need to improve..........)

1. _____ by _____ Yes

2. _____ by _____ Yes

3. _____ by _____ Yes

4. _____ by _____ Yes

5. _____ by _____ Yes

6. _____ by _____ Yes

Day 4

'The first four Minutes . . . . .'

Much research has been conducted, over the years, in how we build and maintain our relationships. Part of this extensive data and analysis, centres around the first time we meet people - *'The First Four Minutes'*.

Whether we like it or not, and whether we work at it consciously or not, we form impressions of each other, as soon as we meet.

The analysis argues, with some justification that these *'First Four Minutes'* are crucial in setting the pattern for the rest of the interaction. For instance;

- When interviewing someone for a vacancy, we make our mind up in the **'first four minutes'** – the rest of the interview is spent looking to confirm that 'first impression'.

- When running a meeting, the **'first four minutes'** are crucial in setting the tone for the whole meeting. If it gets off to a bad start – it may not recover!

- When a Partner returns home from work or a trip, the **'first four minutes'** are crucial in setting the tone for the evening.

WHY EXACTLY FOUR MINUTES?

This is not a figure chosen at random. Researchers have observed thousands of people in different contact situations and have found that, on average, it does take **Four Minutes** to establish whether the meeting/relationship should continue or not.

Apart from in the strictly formal stage of contact, people feel 'obliged' to talk to each other for about four minutes. It is only after this that it feels comfortable to part.

Leaders meet many people everyday – formally and informally. (An estimated thirty thousand 1:1 interactions in a working life!)

Effective Leaders pay attention to the many **'First Four Minutes'** they have. This initial impression is vital. All the transactions, word, body language and strokes that take place in the first four minutes, have a special significance. In that short space of time it is decided how the other person perceives you and what future communication will be like.

Here's the Researcher's **FOUR MINUTE TECHNIQUE**

- Smile
- Establish eye contact
- Use the other person's name
- Pay undivided attention
- Show that, without any shadow of doubt, you respect and accept the other person
- Be calm and confident
- Be well-groomed, clean and tidy

Psychological tests have established this to be 'all' that is needed for the other person's total well-being. It sounds simple doesn't it? Go on, try it!!

ACTION:

    Be aware of the 'FOUR MINUTE RULE', today and note what happens

Make reflections on the area covered:

How am I doing with the First Four Minutes?   What will I do to improve?

Be specific!!

Month 1	Month 2	Month 3

Actions I must take:

(Where I need to improve..........)

1. _____ by _____ Yes

2. _____ by _____ Yes

3. _____ by _____ Yes

4. _____ by _____ Yes

5. _____ by _____ Yes

6. _____ by _____ Yes

Day 5

What motivates.......

Every Leader wants motivated people. Whatever walk of life or sector you lead in, you want your staff to be right up there with you. Perhaps, we should take a step back today and think about what motivation really is. Over the years, my experience in many organisations, with many Leaders, tells me that we don't fully grasp what motivation really is.

Motivation is:

Getting someone to **"go beyond their own desires"**

That's it, in a nutshell. Discussions with Leaders indicate that they **know more about** motivation methods – rewards, aspirations etc., than about what motivation really is. Once we fully grasp what motivation really is, it helps us to understand what we need to do, to motivate others. Confusion reigns sometimes. Let me explain.

I have witnessed companies give staff a cash bonus if they arrive on time at work, everyday of the week. The Contract of Employment, which regulates the relationship between the Employer and the Employee requires honest, loyal and faithful service – both ways.
So if the Employee is not arriving on time, everyday, they are breaking the Contract and are therefore open for disciplinary action; not a cash incentive for doing what they should already be doing!

Real motivation of staff is every Leader's responsibility and duty. How do you get people to go beyond their own levels of comfortable effort? It's a personal thing. Here are some 'motivation headlines' – how are you doing?

I'm ok with this

- I have a clear purpose, that motivates me and the Team ☐
- I know my individuals. Where they are at and what will motivate them ☐
- I know 'who' will give extra effort for 'what' additional reward ☐

Now we quickly turn our attention on 'methods of motivation'. Every member of your team will be on one of these levels. Identifying where they are now will give you an idea of what you can do to motivate them to the next level.

Level 1   Money

'Short-term' motivator. The more we have, the more comfortable we are

Level 2   Career progression

Some want to progress in their careers and want to climb the ladder. They will respond to the **challenge of development and be motivated by the opportunity of promotion.**

Level 3   Self-achievement

What the individual thinks they can become. **'What they want to be'** They will give extra effort to personally achieve what they think they can

Action

Choose a couple of your Team today – identify what will motivate them and give it a try!

Make reflections on the area covered:

Select Team Member(s). List their names and **what** you think motivates them.

Then, go ahead and identify **what you will do to motivate them** and **when** you will do it!

Name:	What motivates them? (1, 2 or 3)	What I will do	When I aim to do it	Worked Yes/No

Actions I must take:

(Where I need to improve..........)

1. _____ by _____ Yes

2. _____ by _____ Yes

3. _____ by _____ Yes

4. _____ by _____ Yes

5. _____ by _____ Yes

6. _____ by _____ Yes

Day 6

Changing your people......

Every Leader has, or has had, staff that they would really like to change. If not, completely, by despatching them to another area, then certainly by modifying or changing something about them. Do you recognise the following words:

'He/She would be great, if it wasn't for . . . .'

Effective Leaders influence their staff and are able to 'get change', at least to some degree.

Who would you like to change? Why? Let's think this through together. . . . .
Possibly it's about their performance, or their behaviour.

Performance - recognise under performance by measuring it over a period.

Behaviour - recognise unacceptable behaviour by the 'critical incident' tool.
Identify what they did, didn't do or said by making a note of it (use a diary etc).
Then be prepared to think through what the following issues are.

This model can help. . . .

> **BEHAVIOUR** - What you see or hear from a person – their behaviour.
> 55% of our message is communicated by Body Language
> Our behaviour is driven by our **ATTITUDE.**
>
> **ATTITUDE** - Defined as a **'settled state of mind'** - our 'self talk'
> To change attitude we need to change thinking
> Our attitude is driven by **BELIEFS AND VALUES.**
>
> **BELIEFS AND VALUES** - Our Beliefs and Values are developed over a lifetime, by those who influence us, our parents, educators, etc, etc

Most of us want to see an immediate change in **behaviour**. The easiest way to do this is to threaten someone with punishment. To avoid it, the individual will comply – but notice how it is only short term. The problem soon arises again!

To get longer term change we must be prepared to go beyond their behaviour and discover their attitude. In other words **'FIND OUT WHAT THEY ARE THINKING'** – 'What is their self-talk?
Use questions to get under the surface.

'How are you feeling?   'Why do you feel that?'

Get them to change/modify their thinking and their behaviour will start to change.

GO BEYOND THIS and explore and get them to change their **VALUES and BELIEFS**. If they are willing to modify and change their beliefs, you are **likely to get long-term change.**

In summary: **Everyone, no matter who, can change.** Long term change starts with a change in Values and Beliefs

Remember, if you leave a 'people problem', it will become further ingrained and eventually some future leader will still have the problem – only bigger. That's what has happened to you, isn't it?

ACTION:

> **Identify the person who needs to change and use the above model to improve that person today!**

Make reflections on the area covered:

Who will I select?   What will I do and when?

Month 1	Month 2	Month 3

Actions I must take:

(Where I need to improve..........)

1. _____ by _____ Yes

2. _____ by _____ Yes

3. _____ by _____ Yes

4. _____ by _____ Yes

5. _____ by _____ Yes

6. _____ by _____ Yes

Day 7

A Balanced Leader. . . .

Being balanced can be a dangerous thing! When we are stationary we have much better balance, than when are moving forward. When we are moving we are not as stable – we are prone to fall because we have opened ourselves up to **risk**. Ever learned to ride a bicycle? Stay still and we are less likely to fall off, but riding is about moving forward. Then there is always a chance we may fall off, but it is the only way to learn. It's like that in life and Leadership too.

There is always more danger when we move forward. Think about the last time you introduced change, to any area of your life. You probably felt uncomfortable and to some extent, fearful.

In the work area, however, it's crucial for Leaders to move forward and sometimes become seemingly unbalanced!

John Adair's **THREE CIRCLE MODEL**, helps to clarify what effective Leaders do to stay balanced. Notice how the three circles, inter-relate.

Effective Leaders:

Achieve the **TASK** by looking after the **INDIVDUAL** and developing the **TEAM**
If a Leader focuses, exclusively on one area, they lose their impact on the other two areas.

For example, if you only focus on 'getting the job done' – the **TASK**, you will ignore people and that could cause problems. Have you ever worked for a TASK based Leader? They do not gain the support of their people, who do just enough to avoid punishment or to get the job done.

Effective Leaders balance the three areas – if they go heavy on **TASK** then they need to also spend time with the **INDIVIDUALS** and get the **TEAM** together.

Here are some helpful actions:

        TASK - Set clear objectives, plan and monitor progress

        INDIVIDUAL - Attend to problems and praise people for good effort

        TEAM - Set standards and ensure good communications

ACTION:

    Where's your focus been recently?   Have you covered all three areas?

    Identify actions to 'balance' your Leadership today – and do them!

Make reflections on the area covered:

How long have I been **TASK** focussed in the last 10 working days?

What have I done to motivate **INDIVIDUALS?** Who and how?

Have we had a **TEAM** Meeting of any kind?

Month 1	Month 2	Month 3

Actions I must take:

(Where I need to improve..........)

1. _____ by _____ Yes

2. _____ by _____ Yes

3. _____ by _____ Yes

4. _____ by _____ Yes

5. _____ by _____ Yes

6. _____ by _____ Yes

Day 8

The power of words.......

Research reminds us that 55% of our message is conveyed by our Body Language and gestures. 38% is conveyed by the tone of our voice – leaving 7%, of the message being communicated **by the words!**

A forest fire is started by a little spark! The smallest word can build up or tear down. There is great power in the tongue.

We tend to remember words, which are spoken to us, throughout our lives – the hurtful ones tend to stick easier than the positive ones, particularly if it is from those closest to us

As it is with us, so it is with all the people we will have contact with today. What will you do with your words?

A Leader's words can:

- Build a foundation for life in others.
- Save others from ruining their lives.
- Feed and build others up.
- Create world beaters in your Team.

Or, our words could have the opposite effect!

Generally, people want to be around positive people. We tend to draw away from those who are negative. Watching our language can help us to **stay positive**. Our words give away our attitude, (our mindset/thoughts) and actually indicate what we believe about others and ourselves.

The Team Member who says "I can't", believes deep inside, that they aren't able to rise and complete what they need to do. Their words are a giveaway. Getting them to change their language by using positive words will help to change their mindset (self talk) and eventually their personal belief.
They will then be in a position to achieve what they need to do!

Watching our language (words) can help us to stay positive and be proactive – something which all followers want to see in their Leader.

Change the following statements, from negative to positive…

(Negative)		(Positive)
I can't …	to	I…
They won't…	to	They…
I don't want to...	to	I….

Changing our language into a **proactive** state will enable us to achieve so much more. Researchers estimate that performance and achievement improvements will be in the region of 5000%. That must be of interest to every Leader!

ACTION:

Make a particular effort today to stay positive with your words.

Plant some positive seeds in your talk with others and watch for the results!

Make reflections on the area covered:

What will I do today to stay positive?

Month 1	Month 2	Month 3

Actions I must take:

(Where I need to improve..........)

1. _____ by _____ Yes

2. _____ by _____ Yes

3. _____ by _____ Yes

4. _____ by _____ Yes

5. _____ by _____ Yes

6. _____ by _____ Yes

Day 9

Spend the 80% on the 20%

Effective Leaders get things done - well. So do their Teams and their Individuals.

Time is the only resource we can't buy more of. Once the day has gone, it's gone forever. At the end of this week, you have one week less than you had before you started. What did you achieve? Did you waste any time?

You can't have the seven days back – whatever time you failed to invest is gone forever, maybe even wasted.

Do the following calculations:

MAN		**WOMAN**	
Expected life span	77 years	Expected life span	82 years
Less your age	_____	Less your age	_____
Total	_____	Total	_____
Multiply by 52 =	_____ weeks	Multiply by 52 =	_____ weeks

Your total is the **number of weeks you have left** to live, assuming you go to the expected age.

It may be a sobering thought, depressing even, but it does emphasis, how important a week of your life is.

That's why **a clearly defined purpose is so crucial**.

How we spend our time is also important. We should have clearly defined objectives (targets), which then help us to identify our **PRIORITIES**.

In a work context, it is usually easier to see our targets. The **PARETO PRINCIPLE (80/20)** rule is of enormous help here.

Consider **EFFECTIVENESS** – 'achieving what we set out to do. **PARETO** identifies that:

20% of our objectives will give us 80% of our effectiveness, as shown here

OBJECTIVES	EFFECTIVENESS
1, 2 — **20%**	**80%**
3, 4, 5, 6, 7, 8, 9, 100 — **80%**	**20%**

Notice how spending our time in the *TOP 20%* of our objectives, ensures we get **80% of the results** anticipated. (Effectiveness)

Notice too, how spending our time on the lower tasks gives us only 20% effectiveness!!

Ever go home at night, thinking, "I've worked hard today and don't feel I've achieved anything!"

Reason? You've been pulled into the lower level objectives. Try and delegate lower level tasks.

ACTION:

Identify your TOP 20% objectives and stay in them!

Make reflections on the area covered:

List your objectives - important first then measure the % time you spend in these areas over the next five working days.

1 hour = 12%. Convert your Totals to percentages, for comparison

OBJECTIVE/TASK	Day 1	Day 2	Day 3	Day 4	Day 5	Total	% Rank
Total hours							

At the end of each day, estimate the time spent on each area, as a percentage (%)

(1 hour is about 12%, based on an eight hour day)

At the end of the period, reflect back on your performance.

How much time was in your top 20%, ie Objectives 1, 2, and 3

What do you need to change and when?

What can I delegate? To who? When?

Remember, it's your time and your life. Invest it well!

Actions I must take:

(Where I need to improve..........)

1. _____ by _____ Yes

2. _____ by _____ Yes

DAY 10

Everything rises or falls on Leadership

The success of a Team or Organisation, is down to its Leadership. So too, is its failure. In other words, **'a Team never rises above its Leadership'**

I've experienced many situations, where Leaders have 'inherited' difficult and under-performing Team Members. The real truth is that previous Leaders have not dealt with the problems and issues. The behaviour of the poor performers then becomes even more engrained. In fact, one such employee even boasted to me that she had 'seen off' three Leaders already. The current Leader therefore has a choice: 'deal with it, or leave an even bigger problem for the next Leader'.

Similarly, we all mirror what we see in our Leaders. Our words whisper – our actions shout! If the Leader doesn't do it, neither will their Team. Conversely, Team Members will do what they see, modelled by their Leader.

Here are some 'real life' examples, from organisational life:

1. The Chief Executive refused to wear protective equipment on the machine shop of his company.
   Result: Employees refused to wear protective equipment giving the Supervisors a real problem

2. The Sales Director announced that the Company was to run a 'Customer first' campaign and refused to take a call from a customer.
   Result: Staff didn't take the campaign seriously!!

3. A Managing Director declared in a meeting with all staff that everyone was to follow the company management structure for communicating with each other – except for himself.
   Result: People continued as they always did, which was to short circuit the structure

The common factor is all there – **'your actions speak louder than words'**

Challenge - What have your actions being saying recently?

Having trouble getting people to 'buy in' to certain actions? Why? What are you doing/not doing?

Note a few actions/behaviours from your own performance, over the last few days/weeks:

1. .... Was it Good or Bad?

2. .... Was it Good or Bad?

3. .... Was it Good or Bad?

Remember, as a Leader, your success is your Team's success - and so is its failure.

ACTION:

Choose a message you want to promote, then go and behave accordingly!

Make reflections on the area covered:

How am I doing with the above?   What will I do and when?

Month 1	Month 2	Month 3

Actions I must take:

(Where I need to improve..........)

1. _____ by _____ Yes

2. _____ by _____ Yes

3. _____ by _____ Yes

4. _____ by _____ Yes

5. _____ by _____ Yes

6. _____ by _____ Yes

DAY 11

Go the 'extra mile. . . .'

"If my organisation was littered with extra mile people at every level,
I would have the most successful time ever!" said one Managing Director.

The 'extra mile' concept is well known in Customer Service areas, but it applies to every corner of every organisation. If we can get our Teams and Individuals to adopt this process, **as standard**, we will have an incredible performance, at every level.

The principle applies to 'internal' customers as much as it does to external ones.

Imagine:

> the Accountants giving additional support to individual Managers, helping them 1:1 on a regular basis to preserve costs.

> the Quality Controllers, spending time with Production Teams to solve recurring problems and seeing this as part of their standard approach.

> the Marketing Team taking time out, to really help and support the Sales Team.

Sounds like utopia? Well it is possible, and the way it can happen? **Every Leader must do it** and thereby become a **'model'** for their people. Remember, everyone watches the Leader and to some extent, model their behaviour.

So if Leaders go the extra mile, for their internal customers, so will their staff. If people won't, it's probably that their Leaders that **aren't doing it** in the first place.

If you are a Leader, you are in a privileged and great position to 'go the extra mile'. Others will follow you (in the main), and replicate this to their contacts, who will then replicate it and so on! The possibilities are endless. . .

See, however, that it all starts with you, the Leader. Someone once said,

'Your words whisper, your actions shout'

However, let's be clear that 'going the extra mile' is not about taking over other people's tasks and activities. It's not about doing their job for them. It's not about being an overworked, pushover!!

It is about understanding how extra support or effort from you will result in a better result for them and then the overall Team and Organisation.

ACTION:

> **Identify examples of how you can go the extra mile today?**

> **How have you gone the extra mile previously?**

> **How can you get your staff to 'go the extra mile'?**

Make reflections on the area covered:

How am I doing with the above?   What will I do and when?

Month 1	Month 2	Month 3

Actions I must take:

(Where I need to improve..........)

1. _____ by _____ Yes

2. _____ by _____ Yes

3. _____ by _____ Yes

4. _____ by _____ Yes

5. _____ by _____ Yes

6. _____ by _____ Yes

DAY 12

The Customer Thing...

We all have customers. Without them we don't have a future. We should never forget that they are the people who buy or use our products/services. Mahatma Gandhi reputedly said it well with this quote, that he had hanging up in the Bank where he worked:

> **Customers are not an intrusion to our work - they are the purpose of it. We are not doing them a favour by serving them. They are doing us a favour by allowing us to**

What a challenge this is. It's not hard to find examples when this doesn't happen. We all have our stories:

1. The Shop Assistant who carries on talking to her colleague when she is supposed to be serving you.

2. The Hotel Receptionist, who carries on operating the keyboard, even though you have arrived and just want to get to your room.

3. The Administrator who is too busy to answer the phone, because they are 'in the middle of something'

4. The Sales Person who is not really listening to us and doesn't try to understand our needs.

How do the above examples, or some of your own, make you feel? Undervalued and we don't want to feel undervalued again, so we don't return.

Leaders, I think, have a great duty to ensure that their Teams are Customer/Client focussed.

Remember, followers do what they see and hear their Leaders do. To build a customer focussed Team *you*, the Leader has to:

1. **Highly value the Client/Customer and show it**

2. **Give the Customer every priority**

3. **Praise the Team when they are excellent in this area.
   Review when they are not and ensure that changes are made!**

We all have our successes and failings. People who have a poor experience with your people will tell four times more people than they will, if they have a good experience.

ACTION:

Step back and identify examples how your Team members have dealt with customers over the last ten working days

Were these good or bad?

Not observed any? Suggest you look really hard over the next couple of days!

Make reflections on the area covered:

Are my Team Customer focussed?   How do I know?   How can they improve?

Month 1	Month 2	Month 3

Actions I must take:

(Where I need to improve..........)

1. _____ by _____ Yes

2. _____ by _____ Yes

3. _____ by _____ Yes

4. _____ by _____ Yes

5. _____ by _____ Yes

6. _____ by _____ Yes

DAY 13

Manage yourself. . .

"If you **cannot manage yourself**, how can you manage others?" were the words that shouted out of an article on Personnel Management. If, as Leaders, we can't manage our time, our lives, there is little chance of having a major impact on those around us.

It's true isn't it! Effective Leaders manage:

> ➢ Their stress levels
> ➢ Their time
> ➢ Their relationships, and so on. . .

Life in general, is getting tougher. Change is faster and never ending. There are still only 24 hours in a day – less than that available for us to fulfil our organisation's requirements. Project forward and the pace, of change and the rate of change, will continue to get faster. With it comes increased pressure. Quicker decision making is required, so there is less time to think. Everyone around is becoming more demanding. Most of us, as Leaders, are moving into new areas, where we are finding our skills and knowledge, are not fully applicable anymore. This in turn causes us to worry that our skills set are outdated – some of our better ones may become redundant!

All this adds considerable stress to our lives. Research has shown that biggest pressures are caused by time – or lack of it! Some of our common statements are:

"I never have the time to.. " "Just not enough hours in the day.." "If I had the time, I would.."

The bad news is, there will never be more time available to us. This most important resource (that is what it is!) cannot be stored for a later date. Once the last hour has gone, it's gone forever! What did you get from it? Every second, 86,400 of them, everyday, must be invested so we get a return. One hour of relaxation, properly invested, will give us a great return on reducing our stress levels.

Getting hold of our time will enable us to get hold of our lives. Sounds good? How?

Let's take yesterday as a start. Step back and assume you had eight hours in your working day. Categorise how you spent it under the following headings;

		Helpful	Waste
On my Top 20% of my objectives	___hrs	☐	☐
Meetings	___hrs	☐	☐
1:1 with staff/colleagues	___hrs	☐	☐
Doing jobs/requests for people outside my Department	___hrs	☐	☐
Others	___hrs	☐	☐
Total	**8 hrs**		

Now, get tough with yourself. Tick the helpful or the waste boxes, as appropriate. If you're spending time on WASTE, you'll be going home frustrated; despite lots of effort, with llow results. Do the same today and tomorrow – then get your team doing the same exercise!

ACTION:

Get your staff to review where they spend their time over the next five days

Make reflections on the area covered:

What do I need to improve/adjust?   How and when?

Month 1	Month 2	Month 3

Actions I must take:

(Where I need to improve..........)

1. _____ by _____ Yes

2. _____ by _____ Yes

3. _____ by _____ Yes

4. _____ by _____ Yes

5. _____ by _____ Yes

6. _____ by _____ Yes

DAY 14

The Leader v The Manager

Organisations today require Leaders more than ever. Yet many people with responsibility want to just be Managers. So, what's the difference? Look at the following list.

The Manager:	**The Leader:**
Engages in **day-to-day** activities:	**Formulates long-term** objectives for reforming the system: Plans strategy and tactics.
Maintains and allocates resources.	Acts to **bring about change** in others in line with long-term objectives.
Administers organisational systems	**Innovates** for the entire organisation
Acts within established cultures	**Creates vision** and strives to transform culture.
Uses **transactional** influence: Includes compliance in behaviour using rewards, sanctions, and formal authority	Uses **transformational** influence: Includes change in people's values, attitudes and behaviour

In summary,

> Management is about **organisation/co-ordination/process**. Leadership is about **PEOPLE at all levels**
>
> Some research suggests that consistent Leader behaviour can improve performance by over 2000%!!!

Can you also see that the emphasis of Leadership is about the future, short, medium and long-term. Leaders must spend time focussing on these time frames ant just today. It's crucial.

A Manager, who I have a great deal of respect for, recently studied a spreadsheet, projecting future cash flow levels.

> "I'm working harder than ever, but I didn't see this coming!"

Reason? He was too busy 'managing' – allocating, controlling the day-to-day. He wasn't focussing on the future. Future possibilities, put perspective into today. Hard work and effort are not enough to guarantee success. You know that anyway, don't you?

ACTION:

> **If you haven't already, identify what you expect to happen in the next 12 months.**
>
> **Share it with your Team and Colleagues**

Make reflections on the area covered:

What do you think will happen in the next 12 months?   What will you communicate and to who?

Month 1	Month 2	Month 3

Actions I must take:

(Where I need to improve..........)

1. _____ by _____ Yes

2. _____ by _____ Yes

3. _____ by _____ Yes

4. _____ by _____ Yes

5. _____ by _____ Yes

6. _____ by _____ Yes

DAY 15

Body Language says it all..

We communicate with people 'all the time'. We were designed to relate to other people. If we can't communicate we become isolated. It's not easy to live on our own – we were made to be with others. In a working life we will have in excess of thirty thousand 1:1 discussions!

As reviewed earlier, the message we give is retained/understood by others via:

Words 7%:   Tone 38%:   Body language 55%

People get more of the message by what our Body Language is saying. Try smirking and laughing while you are telling someone that, 'They are the greatest performer you have ever seen' What do you think they will believe more - your words or your gestures?
You got it – our gestures!

Our behaviour is therefore crucial. What messages do we get from Body language? Charlie Chaplin knew. His films have delighted millions of people all over the world. Most of his films were silent, but it didn't matter – he could portray the whole range of human emotions without saying a single word. He was a master of body language.

There are nearly one million body language signals to do with:
- Facial expressions
- Eye contact
- Eye movements
- Gestures with hands and arms
- Distance from others
- Stance and posture
- Direction in which the body is pointing
- Sitting position
- Movements

Body language speaks the truth. Effective Leaders **learn how to use the right gestures** to emphasise the message they are giving.
People use their body language automatically, and they use it all the time. If you know how to interpret body language, you can make a good guess at what others are thinking…what they really mean and are feeling. If someone tells a lie, their body language will usually give them away. But you must be careful not to isolate one action and base your assumption on that alone. A person who has her arms folded may not be being defensive, she might just be cold! A person might physically be unable to display body language, e.g. because he has arthritis.
People from different countries and cultures use different types of body language. Women and men may use different signs, or variations of the same sign – it might even depend on what they are wearing. So remember that you cannot generalise or assume too much.

ACTION:

> **Be aware of your own and other gestures, today**
>
> **Think about an important message you are going to give someone. What gestures will you use?**

Make reflections on the area covered:

What gestures can you use to re-inforce your message? What gestures do others use?

Month 1	Month 2	Month 3

Actions I must take:

(Where I need to improve..........)

1. _____ by _____ Yes

2. _____ by _____ Yes

3. _____ by _____ Yes

4. _____ by _____ Yes

5. _____ by _____ Yes

6. _____ by _____ Yes

DAY 16

Who will you influence today?

Leaders are in the influence game. Management is more transactional – planning, co-ordinating, dealing with the day-to-day. Leadership embraces these activities and adds a vital ingredient - vision - the future state required. Without a vision, the Leader is just on a walk. Leaders are going somewhere! They communicate this to those who are following. Leaders are influential.

Why not try the 'acid test' of Leadership, today? Take a paper and write down the names of those who you are truly leading. Be honest. If you have written some names down - great. Now examine and identify **why** you are 'influencing' them, to follow you.

Amongst definitions, influence is:

"The capacity to be a compelling force on the actions, behaviour and opinions of others"

The truly effective Leader has the ability to influence others and get 'buy in' and 'the extra mile' support. If the Leader is relying on his/her authority within the organisation, alone, their followers will do 'just enough'. Influential Leaders are able to get that additional effort - even when it's not asked for! Why? Because they are able to influence people! This includes their followers, people at the same level and above. This is the true 360° Leader.

Here are some of the things that will assist you to raise your influence levels;

> Ensure you become competent within the area of your operation. Don't confuse experience with competence. Experience may accelerate your competence level, but competence is about performing to standard 'on-the-job' today.

> The next quality is to do with the Leader's honesty, courage, integrity – (doing what they say). These basic principles, if they are present, will elicit respect and give the Leader opportunities to have impact.

> **COMMUNICATION** - in capital letters, because competence and honesty are about you. Communication is about others. We communicate not only through our words and tone, but through our behaviour and gestures (Body Language).

Effective communications help us to be a 'people person'
Make people laugh and they enjoy being in your company.
Use positive words - be positive - people like being around positive people. They gain energy and encouragement. These things will help them to like you. Important?
Yes! They will do more for someone they like, than for someone they don't.
So to build your influence;

"Competence, character, communication and the greatest of these is communication"

ACTION:

> **How are you doing with the following influences? Tick if ok**
>
> **Competence ☐   Honesty, courage, integrity ☐   Communication ☐**
>
> **If not ticked, it's time to put it right**

Make reflections on the area covered:

How am I doing with the above?   What will I do and when?

Month 1	Month 2	Month 3

Actions I must take:

(Where I need to improve..........)

1. _____ by _____ Yes

2. _____ by _____ Yes

3. _____ by _____ Yes

4. _____ by _____ Yes

5. _____ by _____ Yes

6. _____ by _____ Yes

DAY 17

Timing is crucial . . . .

In many areas of life, timing is crucial. Whether it's a musical performance, sporting event or even trying to catch a ball – correct timing is crucial.

It's so with Leadership. Experience teaches us that the immediate time is not always the best and most appropriate time to tackle some of the issues that we face. Here are some working examples:-

➢ A member of your team is angry with a certain situation. They are showing it by their behaviour towards others. **Now is not the best time** to try and get to the bottom of the problem. There is too much emotion about.

➢ Team members are in a very busy period at work. **Now is not the best time** to engage them in the longer term vision that you have.

There are some instances, however, when now <u>is</u> the best time to address issues:

➢ A member of the Team flagrantly flouts company procedures in their work. **Now is a time** to emphasise that this is not acceptable – even if they are busy.

➢ A Team member questions what's being done. **Now is a great time** to expand the discussions to get their views – who knows what improvements may follow.

Great Leaders understand that timing is important. When to introduce an issue requires planning. It may be the right thing to do, but people have to be 'ready for it'. There was a man in Jewish history who wanted to rebuild the walls of the capital of the Nation, Israel. Jerusalem was a sacred and honoured place. When he heard about its ruins he was determined to do something about it. History tells us that he got the commission in December, but didn't put his plan into action until April. We're not sure what he was waiting on, but we can extrapolate . . . .

➢ He was making sure he was clear about what needed doing.

➢ He was becoming 'internally' ready for the challenge.

➢ He was waiting for others to become ready, affecting their mental and emotional states.

➢ He was waiting for the right season (weather wise) for the rebuilding to take place.

Recognising the right time to move is crucial in successful outcomes. Actually, history tells us, that when he pressed the button, the job was done in record time – because people, the season and the opportunity were all 'right'.

A key question for all Leaders is 'when do we move?'

How does asking at the right time increase your chances of success?

ACTION:

    Reflect on some of the issues you have moved on, over the last month.

    Was the timing right? Why?

Make reflections on the area covered:

List the recent issue(s)?   Was the timing right?

Why was it?   Why wasn't it?

Month 1	Month 2	Month 3

Actions I must take:

(Where I need to improve..........)

1. _____ by _____ Yes

2. _____ by _____ Yes

3. _____ by _____ Yes

4. _____ by _____ Yes

5. _____ by _____ Yes

6. _____ by _____ Yes

DAY 18

A Leader's courage…..

Courageous Leaders change things - significant progress can't be made without courage. Whenever you see significant progress in a Team or an organisation, it's because the Leader(s) have made decisions with courage. It's a crucial ingredient and it's infectious. Courage levers commitment from followers – it inspires them to be courageous too!

Let's be clear – a Leadership position doesn't give any person courage. Rather, courage gives them a Leadership position.

We will all face tough decisions, especially in today's environments. It goes with the territory, but recognising these truths will help:

1. Courage begins within us.

We have to win the battle within ourselves. Our first reaction to challenge, may well be to crumble inside - to want to flee from the issues.
Winning the inner battle, where we determine to face the issues square on, is crucial.

Martin Luther King Junior said,

> "The measure of a man is not where he stands in moments of comfort and convenience, but where he stands in times of challenge and controversy."

2. Your life expands in proportion to your courage.

Courage opens doors and that's one of its most precious benefits.
If you don't grow, your Team and organisation stagnate, then die. There are many examples around us. Success comes with Leaders 'stepping up to the plate'
So, the courageous Leader steps forward to face the situation.

Leaders need courage to make decisions such as:

- Dealing with a conflict in the team, not smoothing it over
- Committing resources to developing the business
- Taking the organisation into new and bigger markets
- And so on…

Courage leads us to greater levels of success. It takes us out of our comfort zones. Expanding our lives into new areas usually creates feelings of fear. Go too far and we may even feel panic. That's exactly when courage needs to kick in.
Remember too, that fear is a natural reaction, but it doesn't need to dictate our responses.

Someone once said,
> 'Feel the fear and do it anyway!

Courage is required at all levels of Leadership. Remember, it inspires others. In today's climate, whatever sector you operate in, you will be required to make courageous decisions. Courage defines who the real Leaders are and it is unlikely that you will develop, without courage. It will make you the Leader you need to be.

ACTION:

What decisions are you facing now? Do you need to get a "fresh wind" of courage? Determine within yourself that you will do it!

Make reflections on the area covered:

What issues do I need to resolve?   What will I do and when?

Month 1	Month 2	Month 3

Actions I must take:

(Where I need to improve..........)

1. _____ by _____ Yes

2. _____ by _____ Yes

3. _____ by _____ Yes

4. _____ by _____ Yes

5. _____ by _____ Yes

6. _____ by _____ Yes

DAY 19

Coach for success

Managers and Leaders, collectively, have millions of opportunities for developing their people, to enable them to bring a better and greater contribution to their organisation. The problem is, they don't recognise it.

Training, particularly if it's away from the workplace, is expensive. The direct costs, loss of contribution from the work area, make 'off-the-job' training, prohibitive. **Coaching,** however, seeks to use the **'everyday work opportunities'** as a vehicle for developing people. It's usually 'in house', job related and very 'client focused'.

In my experience, I have found that training and development interventions for people are really well received. If you help to develop someone you are investing into their lives, their future. People don't forget that personal investment! True, it helps the organisation reap improvements and so it should, but skills and capabilities are very personal and they are for life. Being involved in developing people enables you to lever greater levels of commitment, because of what you have done for them personally. Bluntly, if you don't develop your people, as a Leader, you are missing out on masses of talent and commitment that is within your people.

Coaching is a great and effective way to developing your people.

We coach to:

- Correct under performance
- Develop people's potential

Here's a simple tool you can use today! It's called **T.O.D.E**. After recognising there is a need for coaching, discuss it with the 'Client' (Team Member) and identify:

Targets - Set a clear improvement target. Make it:
"**SPECIFIC – ACHIEVABLE – MEASURABLE**"

e.g. To sell *1000* of *product A* by *31/12/xx*

Opportunities - Now look for the opportunity for the training/development. This may be arranging time in another part of the organisation. It may include structured training.

Do it - Be clear about the achievement dates set and ensure you are both committed to them. Agree a review date.

Evaluate - Review with the Client, what has happened and be prepared To update/reset Targets (**T**)

A final word on the effective Coach's behaviour:

➢ **Be positive**
➢ **Listen**
➢ **Lead the Client through the process**

ACTION:

Go on – coach somebody today – you won't regret it.

Make reflections on the area covered:

Who shall I coach?   What do they need to be able to do?

Plan it and do it!!

Month 1	Month 2	Month 3

Actions I must take:

(Where I need to improve..........)

1. _____ by _____ Yes

2. _____ by _____ Yes

3. _____ by _____ Yes

4. _____ by _____ Yes

5. _____ by _____ Yes

6. _____ by _____ Yes

Day 20

Personal attitude – how important!!

Everybody and I mean everybody, watches the Leader like a hawk. They are listening to the Leader's words. They are watching everything. A Leader cannot hide. They are on show all the time.
Effective Leaders are good communicators. They have learned, (yes communication is a skill that can be learned and developed), how to get the message across.
How is this done?
Through your words – they are important. Reactive language is always easier than proactive language. Being reactive in our language leads to an average life.

Here are some examples of reactive phrases and their proactive equivalents:

Reactive	Proactive
I can't. .	I can. .
They won't allow that. .	I will convince them to by. .
I won't. .	I Will. .

Who would you rather be around? Positive people who talk as though they can, or negative people who think they can't. I know my answer to that!
Research tells us that our behaviour (body language), communicates over half of the message. That's more than the words we speak. Our gestures are very important. Again, we must ensure that in every interaction we reinforce our words, with positive body actions. (Behaviour)
These include:

    Smiling: Listening: Using an open posture

Many of these gestures are to do with our faces - our eyes and mouth being critical. One of my Leaders, from years ago would grimace when I mentioned an idea. He did this three times. Then I decided to stop bringing new ideas - his face said it all. What a great loss!
Think about the last few interactions you have had, as a Leader. It could be 'one to one' or at a meeting.

> **How positive and proactive was your language?**
> **What did your gestures communicate?**

Before we finish, let's review what drives our words and behaviours. Any ideas?
Well, majorly it's our attitude! We can all recognise a good or bad attitude, but we struggle to define what attitude really is. **Attitude is a settled state of mind (or thinking).** Therefore, if we think something, it comes out in our talk or behaviour. e.g. 'If you don't think you can, you probably won't' If you think you can't do things, you won't succeed'. It's as basic as that!

In a survey of 500 Senior Managers, 94% attributed success to ATTITUDE more than any other basic ingredient. The Carnegie Institute surveyed 10,000 employees and their results indicated that 85% of success was due to attitude – 15% down to technical competence.
I've never met a successful Leader, with a 'bad' attitude.
Attitude determines how high our leadership rises.
Because people are watching us – OUR ATTITUDE determines the ATTITUDE OF OTHERS!!

ACTION:
> **Review your attitude, (thinking or 'self talk') over the last 24 hours.**
>
> **Has it been positive or negative?**

Make reflections on the area covered:

List the negative and positive behaviours you have used over the last few days?

What will I do and when?

Month 1	Month 2	Month 3

Actions I must take:

(Where I need to improve..........)

1. _____ by _____ Yes

2. _____ by _____ Yes

3. _____ by _____ Yes

4. _____ by _____ Yes

5. _____ by _____ Yes

6. _____ by _____ Yes

Day 21

Communicating to win

There are many forms of communication; in business and in life, generally. Typical descriptions of communication would include:

- 'The passing of information between two people'
- 'The transfer of ideas between two people or groups of people'
- 'Transferring a thought or message to another party, so that it might be understood'

One of the more useful descriptions would be:

> **"Communication is the transfer of information from one person to another <u>resulting in action</u>."**

Consider this model:

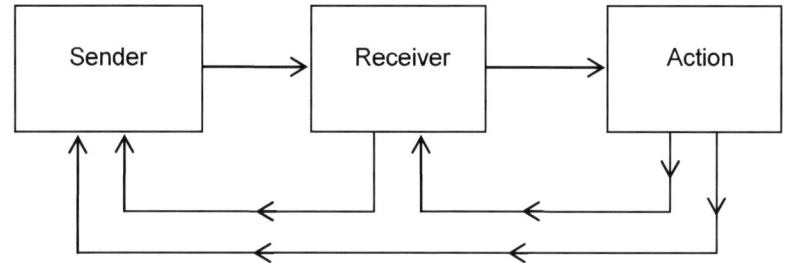

Notice how the feedback loops work. The Sender and the Receiver both get feedback from the action. If the required action is met, successful communication has been achieved. If the action isn't right don't just blame the Receiver. The Sender and Receiver can also clarify the message, before the action.

THE IMPORTANCE OF COMMUNICATIONS:

Communication is a key Leadership skill. Good communication has great effects in:

> *Building trust between all people*
>
> *Implementing change. We can clearly explain what is required and why*
>
> *Achieving the required results*

In summary:

People are encouraged to perform at a higher level if they **understand** decisions, which affect them and the **reasons** for those decisions. It is a clear Leadership requirement to always communicate clearly, with those in their Team, their Colleagues and their Seniors

Effective communications must not be left to 'ad-hoc' or casual methods.

ACTION:

How are you doing with your communications?

Make reflections on the area covered:

How can I make my communications better and more effective?   What will I do and when?

Month 1	Month 2	Month 3

Actions I must take:

(Where I need to improve..........)

1. _____ by _____ Yes

2. _____ by _____ Yes

3. _____ by _____ Yes

4. _____ by _____ Yes

5. _____ by _____ Yes

6. _____ by _____ Yes

Day 22

Balance your life...

Living today is more pressured than ever. If you are a Leader within an organisation, then the pressures and the stress levels are even higher. How we handle that stress will have a great bearing on our outputs - our effectiveness.
The signs of stress are usually quite easy to identify. We see them in people, everyday. Think about the people you have regular contact with. Are they under stress?
Researchers tell us that some of the stress symptoms include:

> - **Continual tiredness - usually worsened by poor sleep patterns.**
> - **Moodiness and withdrawal**
> - **Irrational behaviour - people do things 'which don't make sense'.**
> - **Physical ailments - complaints of aches, pains and worse!**

Make no mistake about it – stress is a killer and the general levels of stress look set to continue to increase as the organisation's requirements increase and available resources decrease.
People in general, but particularly Leaders, must empower themselves to ensure they have 'coping strategies,' to help them deal with their personal stress levels. Remember, followers are watching their Leader – there is no hiding place. If we allow our responses to flow from our stress induced life we can do massive damage to our people and our relationships.

Think, for instance, of the Leader who withdraws from the Team for a period.
Think, for instance, of the Leader who 'snaps' at a Team member, because their tiredness reduces their patience and they just snapped.

If we do not 'capture' our stress levels we will harm ourselves too. We easily descend into 'burn out' and if that isn't caught we end up with a breakdown.
Psychologists tell us that the human body does need some stress. It helps us to perform in life, but the crucial thing is to make sure that we are handling it well. We need to balance our lives between the following three areas, circled below.

If we allow one of the areas to dominate the other two, we are allowing stress levels to rise.
Here are some practical examples:

1. Spend too much time at work and we suffer, as will as our family.
   We feel guilty about not maintaining these close relationships
2. Someone I know spent long hours at work, (not always productive), and had high expectations for his family life and social commitments.
He didn't leave time for himself. He experienced 'burn out'.
The practical approach to controlling our stress level, is to 'balance the three areas'.

- **Look after yourself** – physically, emotionally, spiritually.

Ensure you give personal time to yourself on a daily basis you are your best product.

- **Keep work in perspective** – remember it's not meant to be, 'the be all and end all'.

Ensure you know and keep in your **PRIORITIES**. *(See 80/20 on Day 9)*

- **Enjoy your family and social life.**

Relax and keep your focus wide – enjoy what you like doing.
By balancing the three areas, you will feel in control. Feel in control and your performance will be outstanding.

ACTION:
How are you doing in the three areas?   *Self: Work: Family/Social*

Make reflections on the area covered:

Which area(s) do I need to improve?   What will I do and when?

Month 1	Month 2	Month 3

Actions I must take:

(Where I need to improve..........)

1. _____ by _____ Yes

2. _____ by _____ Yes

3. _____ by _____ Yes

4. _____ by _____ Yes

5. _____ by _____ Yes

6. _____ by _____ Yes

Day 23

Three Levels of Leadership

When it comes to Leadership, we've read the books, studied the 'new' approaches, discovered some useful, clear Leadership principles. Some as old as the hills!!
Some are not so new, but still valid.
The Three Levels of Leadership builds on work developed by Dr John Maxwell, where his process enables a Leader to see which level they are operating from and the consequences of that style.

Here is an overview of the *'THREE LEVELS OF LEADERSHIP'*

Each Level has its own specific issues, benefits and disadvantages. We always start at the lower levels and work up. Effective, influential Leaders work through each Level. As you move up the Levels, the deeper, more solid your Leadership with people, at all levels, will be. Each Level climbed by the Leader adds another reason why your people follow.

THE LEVEL 1 LEADER (L1)   POSITION

The lowest level of Leadership – conferred by the Organisation.
The **L1** Leader operates off their **POSITION**. This gives them 'rights'. This position is the basic entry level and is based upon the privileges of the position.
New Leaders start at **L1** and have about 100 days 'honeymoon' period, before others expect to see results and outcomes.
People follow **L1** Leaders, 'because they have to'. Members will give minimum effort, time and commitment. **L1** Leaders often use intimidation to gain required actions.

THE LEVEL 2 LEADER (L2)   PERSON

The **L2** Leader leads predominantly, by relationships, effectively developed with others. This **PERSON CENTRED** approach recognises that we need and are made, to relate to others!!
They have moved from the L1 position and are secure enough to build relationships. At this **L2** level, followers don't care how much you know, rather, it's how much you care, that counts. They follow because they want to. Extra effort and 'going the extra mile' is the norm from the Team members for **L2** Leaders. People like the **L2** Leader and may even become fiercely loyal.
At the **L2** Level, however, Leaders may abuse their followers.

THE LEVEL 3 LEADER (L3)   PERFORMANCE

Results are great and at this level they are in abundance. Good results come from effective **PERFORMANCE**, from the Team Members. The **L3** Leader is now through the two lower levels of Leadership and is starting to see real results appear. **L3** is a phenomenal position to be in. Winning Teams win and win and win. The **L3** leader sees this happening time and time again. They have added real motivation to their relationships, identifying the different abilities in Team Members and allowing them to operate in key strength areas.

ACTION:

        Which level are you on? Be honest.

        To go to the next Level - What do you need to do?

Make reflections on the area covered:

What's the next Level?   What will I do and when?

Month 1	Month 2	Month 3

Actions I must take:

(Where I need to improve..........)

1. _____ by _____ Yes

2. _____ by _____ Yes

3. _____ by _____ Yes

4. _____ by _____ Yes

5. _____ by _____ Yes

6. _____ by _____ Yes

Day 24

The power of Teams and Individuals!!

It goes without saying that every effective Leader builds and develops a great Team around them. The output of Teams is obviously greater than that of a person operating alone. This is, 'The law of productivity'. Essentially, how much the Team produces is down to a number of factors.

A healthy Team must be, amongst other things:

1. **Balanced - a right blend of skills and personalities**
2. **Clearly focussed, with every member buying into clearly defined objectives/targets**
3. **Have a good blend of Team roles**

Extensive research by many writers, have opened up to us, what it takes to become a 'high performing Team' We think immediately of Team Roles as prescribed by Belbin. A simplified model for the mix of Team Roles, required to make a Team effective is:

THINKER - Someone who brings carefully weighed ideas.
Thinkers also like detail and information

LEADER - Not necessarily the official leader, but someone who is keen to ensure the direction/purpose is clear to all

CARER - The person who cares about the people and relationships within the Team

DOER - Someone who engages Team members to 'get on with it'.
They are **action people**, who don't always want to stop and think

Research tells us, a successful Team needs a blend of all these roles. For example the Team need to be action focussed **(DOER)**, but also need to use the right information/data **(THINKER).** If these two get into conflict, as they will, the Team requires harmony and understanding **(CARER).** Think of how poor a Team is without a **LEADER**!

Before we leave this subject, much has been said about the need for every member to be committed to the purpose. This is crucial. It goes without saying. However, Paul Scanlan of Bradford, England brought a further thought on this subject.
He stressed that every Team, at sometime, needs to have someone who does something that is *'BRILLIANT'*. We see it in sport. Every Striker needs support from a Team and they occasionally produce 'something', that is a brilliant skill, to win the match. The Batsman who scores a brilliant innings. The fielder with a match winning catch. The Research Team Member who suddenly has a 'Eureka moment'. The Sales-person who pulls an incredible sale off!
Our Teams should never swamp individual talent and ability. Winning Leaders give room for this to happen.
Paul said,
"There may be no 'I' in Team, but there are five in "Individual Brilliance!"

My sentiments entirely!!

Action

Think about the balance in your Team.

Have you got the Thinker/Leader/Carers/Doers?

Make reflections on the area covered:

What Team Roles do I have?	What Team Roles do I need?	Now what?
Month 1	Month 2	Month 3

Actions I must take:

(Where I need to improve..........)

1. _____ by _____ Yes

2. _____ by _____ Yes

3. _____ by _____ Yes

4. _____ by _____ Yes

5. _____ by _____ Yes

6. _____ by _____ Yes

DAY 25

Credibility is a must...

Ever worked for, or with someone, who has little credibility with their colleagues? What were the day-to-day effects? For a Leader, losing credibility presents massive problems!
Integrity is doing and being what we say and believe. If we are not consistent in this area people will see it and some even go as far as calling us hypocrites.
Credibility is acknowledging that someone is 'worthy of belief', ie 'trustworthy'. If a Leader is not seen as trustworthy or believable, their influence levels are dramatically reduced. Life becomes even more difficult. Colleagues will not commit to their Leader or the required actions.

How can a Leader get into such a dire predicament? Here are a few ways:

Not behaving as they are telling others to. Effective, credible Leaders live out the things they are promoting to their followers.

Not keeping their word obviously springs to mind. Every promise honoured builds relationships - promises not delivered on, weakens relationships. We have a relationship bank. Deposits are made when we do as we promised. Withdrawals are made when we break our word. We have different levels of value with different people. Leaders need to go out of their way to make deposits, as one day, they will do something that makes a withdrawal. If there's no credit in there, it's bankruptcy!

Being selfish. A Leader needs to be seen as unselfish.
Getting people to work for the Leader's vision alone, will cause loss of credibility. Leaders are there primarily to 'add value' to the people around them.
I once worked for a Manager, who clearly took credit at the higher level for some of my achievements. Imagine the effect that had on me!

Breaking confidences. Once a Leader breaks a confidence, people will not be willing to share things in the future. Trust is easily destroyed, even though it's taken a long while to build up.

Here are some thoughts on how we can protect and build our credibility:

1.	**Be consistent**	-	Be the same person with everybody
2.	**Choose right**	-	Make decisions on how they will benefit others
3.	**Credit others**	-	Be quick to recognise the efforts of others
4.	**Character**	-	Work hard on integrity – not image

Action

Review the last ten working days?

Have you improved your credibility or destroyed it?

Why not ask around!

Make reflections on the area covered:

How am I doing with my credibility?   What will I do and when?

Month 1	Month 2	Month 3

Actions I must take:

(Where I need to improve..........)

1. _____ by _____ Yes

2. _____ by _____ Yes

3. _____ by _____ Yes

4. _____ by _____ Yes

5. _____ by _____ Yes

6. _____ by _____ Yes

DAY 26

"Stay ahead of the game..."

I think it's true to say that no Leader is the "finished article". There is always room for improvement. Effective Leaders are always looking to learn and develop. It's a daily requirement. This attitude towards personal development ensures:

- We are constantly in touch with the changing environments, in which we exist.

- We are constantly challenged about our own levels of competence.

- We provide a 'role model' for our followers - they get the message that ongoing personal development is crucial.

- We are able to "stay ahead of the game". In other words we see what's likely to challenge us in the future. Good Leaders look ahead and see what's coming.

The areas in which we operate are likely to be changing at a greater pace than ever before. If they are not, they are probably dying! The pace of change is getting faster. Not going with these changes will severely affect our organisation's performance and health. Failure doesn't just happen and it's mainly the fault of Leaders when it does!

How we respond to these changes is crucial. One Leadership writer encourages Leaders to consider how they spend their time to ensure they "stay ahead" of the game.

70% of our time	-	Spend it on our strengths - the areas we do well in
25% of our time	-	Spend it on the new areas we identify as crucial to future success
5% of our time	-	Spend it on the weak areas. The key is to minimise this area as much as possible. This can be done by delegating the associated activities

Lets quickly concentrate on the 25% area - developing new things.

If you want to get better you must keep changing and improving, which means stepping into new areas. If you dedicate time to new things, related to your strength areas, your growth will be assured. I've found that some of the following are particularly useful in this area:

1. **Review the areas as thoroughly as possible.**
   Read, study, visit exhibitions, websites etc and seriously review the content against your own environment. Get at least one new idea from each area and implement it.

2. **Find a Mentor.**
   Someone who's travelled the road before you. Arrange regular meetings always ensure you "take a contribution".

3. **Set clear personal development targets.**
   Make them **S**pecific: **A**chievable: **M**easureable

ACTION:

   What areas are changing and what do you need to do 'stay ahead'

   Why not complete the Personal Development Plan to help

LEADERSHIP DEVELOPMENT PLAN

Complete the boxes with your thoughts.
Start at your Personal Vision and then work through your **Strengths and Weaknesses**. Then identify the **Opportunities and Threats**.
List the Skills Required and the Activities you need to be involved in! Indicate too some target dates against the activities identified.

Strengths

Opportunities

Skills required:

Personal Vision

In five years I will:

Weaknesses:

Threats:

Activities I need to do/be involved in:

Day 27
The loneliness of a Leader…

Being a Leader can be very lonely!
Talking to Dave recently, clarified this. He is a real Visionary. He sees and thinks well into the future, in front of everyone else in his organisation – that's why he's the Leader. His complaint to me was, however, that he always seemed to be out there on his own. No one else was grasping his vision, or his intentions.
'I turn around and there's no one near. I'm on my own most of the time!'
Most Leaders feel lonely at one time or another. It is inevitable. It isn't unnatural and it certainly isn't wrong. Most Leaders feel sometimes that they are 'on their own'. Often, the inability of those close to us to fully understand and support us at key moments merely increases the pain!! The real issue for us as Leaders is what to do with the feelings and the perceived loneliness.
Actions that will help to reduce a Leader's loneliness

1. **Find a Mentor**

    Someone who you can talk to, (candidly) and share thoughts and feelings. This person does not need to be intimately involved in the organisation. Actually, it is better if they are not!
    You can bounce ideas off them and because they are not closely involved, they can engage in discussions from a unique viewpoint. Do they need to be older? Not necessarily, but meetings need to be regular. These will dispel feelings of isolation!

2. **Communicate your Vision more effectively.**

    A frustrated Leader I was speaking to recently said,

    > 'People bring me ideas which aren't in line with where we are going!'

    When I opened a directed discussion with him, it became clear to him that the 'off-line' suggestion was actually his fault. If people don't know the journey, blame the driver!
    Incidentally, if he showed his frustration, it is unlikely that he will get further suggestions from that Team Member.
    Followers need to have the vision consistently reinforced and breaking it down in smaller steps will enable them to grasp it and buy into it quicker. Eventually, there will be others who talk the same vision! Two-way dialogue reduces loneliness!

3. **Identify those in the Team who are the early, positive adopters**.

    Spend time with these people; communicate your hopes and let them add to it. Remember they are with the Team when you are not. They could become your Champions and every cause needs champions!

4. **Don't allow your vision to be all life encompassing.**

    Keep your life balanced, personal, social and work.
    Not so long ago, I went for a meal with Colin, who is seeing good growth and success in his organisation. He couldn't talk about anything else. I was bored by the time the main course was served!
    Leaders should give those around them a break – and themselves too.

Action:

>Lonely? What do you need to do? 1,2,3,4, or a combination?

Make reflections on the area covered:

Which do you need?   What will I do and when?

Month 1	Month 2	Month 3

Actions I must take:

(Where I need to improve..........)

1. _____ by _____ Yes

2. _____ by _____ Yes

3. _____ by _____ Yes

4. _____ by _____ Yes

5. _____ by _____ Yes

6. _____ by _____ Yes

DAY 28

Servant Leadership!!

What appears to be a contradiction in terms, has at the heart of it, some powerful principles. Leaders, it goes without saying, must have a clear vision and purpose. These crucial elements give security to those who are following and give the Leader considerable influence. Another crucial, yet less publicised, purpose of a Leader is to help those around them to recognise and fulfil their potential. Some research indicates that an organisation uses just 10% of a person's potential. One Manager, challenged by this statistic said,

> 'We're paying for the whole body, why not use it!'

The essence of the comment is true. Our people come into our organisation on a daily basis and perform to a level of expectation, set by their Leaders. People tend to do what you measure, not what you expect. Leaders set the tone, the rhythm and the performance levels required – followers comply!

The **'Servant Leader'** approach turns the direction of support on it's head. Instead of saying 'follow me', it's saying,

> 'How can I help you, to improve your performance, to meet the agreed vision and targets?'

The traditional hierarchy of organisations, is 'top down'. Servant Leadership, reverses this and places those at the operational level, as the most important.
See the diagram:

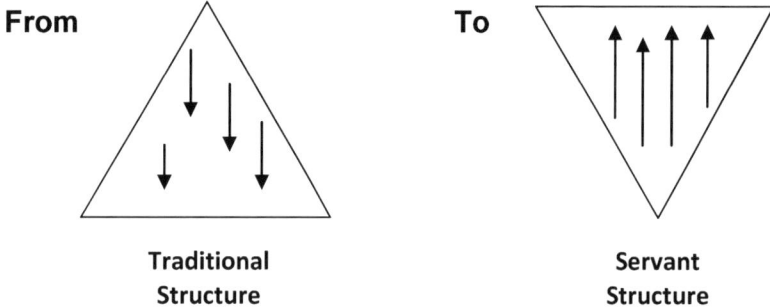

Higher Level Leaders are serving their people, who have become **the** Very Important Person (VIP's!) It looks good on paper – it's fantastically powerful in practice. The Senior Leaders have become the lowest level as they seek to serve the people above them. At the very top of the inverted structure are the employees who have direct contact with those the organisation is trying to serve. (Customers) Everyone is focussed on their Customers receiving the best service, the best product, the best everything. That's the way for any organisation to survive and grow.

If the Leaders are prepared to 'go the extra mile' for the people they are responsible for, those people will go the extra mile for their subordinates. Eventually, those with front-line responsibilities for Customers will by normal operation, also 'go the extra mile'.

There is something very powerful about serving others. It elevates the servant in the eyes of those being served. I've heard it said that to become influential you have to become big. I rather believe that your greatness will be determined by the depth of your service.

Action:

> **Is 'Servant Leadership' truly present in your organisation?**
>
> **What's the next step for you?**

Make reflections on the area covered:

Select some your Team and start to 'serve them', in line with the above?

What will I do and when?

Month 1	Month 2	Month 3

Actions I must take:

(Where I need to improve..........)

1. _____ by _____ Yes

2. _____ by _____ Yes

3. _____ by _____ Yes

4. _____ by _____ Yes

5. _____ by _____ Yes

6. _____ by _____ Yes

Day 29

Different people – different support

Variety is the spice of life! This is so true with people - the people who work for us.
Here are some facts:

- There's only one you and me. No two have the same finger prints, DNA.

- We are all incredibly made, with massive potential

- We sneeze at 37 mph!

- If we could harness the human brain to the national power grid, it would light a city the size of Birmingham in the UK for 24 hours!

- If computer programmes could develop a programme to do what the human brain can do, even in these days of miniaturisation, the computer would be the size of Big Ben in London and would take all the water from the River Thames to 'cool it down'

At work however, how much of this potential is unrecognised and unused. One study I saw, reckoned on about 10% of our potential being used. If that is way out, it's unlikely to be more than 20%! It's the same with our computer systems. We tend to use the same 10% over and over again.

How do you see your staff – your major resource? It's true not everybody has the same potential or ability. I guess the trick is, to recognise who has the potential and the willingness to use it.
Some of our individuals need a great deal of support, others don't.
This can be summarised as follows:

Committed:
>Those who are totally committed to the Leader and the aims of the organisation. They are self-starters, who are willing to take responsibility. They will be the next 'official' Leaders to be appointed. **Look for ways of developing them and promote them!**

Interested:
>The next level down. Usually these workers do an adequate job. They can be left to work conscientiously and perform to the correct level. Look for ways of motivating them by identifying what really turns them on!

Uninterested:
>The people who shouldn't really have a job with you at all. They take masses of support, time and effort in directing and checking. They have to be coerced and pushed. If you don't deal with them now, the problems will get bigger and eventually the next Leader will have the same headache, only bigger.
>What should I do? Consider the three 'T's: Train, Transfer or Terminate.

You can probably even put names against the different levels listed.
The key is;
- Treat people appropriately by identifying what level they are at.
- Encourage people to move to the next level.

Action: **Who do you need to 'work on' this week?**

Make reflections on the area covered:

Who do I need to work on??   What will I do and when?

Month 1	Month 2	Month 3

Actions I must take:

(Where I need to improve..........)

1. _____ by _____ Yes

2. _____ by _____ Yes

3. _____ by _____ Yes

4. _____ by _____ Yes

5. _____ by _____ Yes

6. _____ by _____ Yes

Day 30

The power of potential - if it's used...

Most, if not all Senior Leaders, will openly declare that,

'People are our most important resource'

We will probably share that view too, but in my experience, many people I speak to at all levels of the organisation feel that their people could be contributing more. What stops people performing?
One key area is the lack of motivation – their Leader is not inspiring them

The organisation's procedures and processes – developed with good intent, but they can, in some cases, lever effort downwards.

I recently spent just one hour with an individual. He was fairly demotivated and yet was totally re-energised, as he went away. How did that happen? I got him to focus and identify what was inside him. When he started to uncover his true passion about his life, his disposition totally changed. You will have someone similar in your Team/Organisation, who is in the same position. This type of worker is unfortunately fairly typical in the world of work.
Using the following process will help and I can more or less guarantee the outcome!

1. **Help the individual to discover what they think their purpose is.**
   Question them, (don't put words into their mouths). What excites them?
   I spoke to an individual who was coasting along in the Purchasing. When we started focussing on her future, she switched on. Her body language changed as she confessed her preferred job was in Sales! Very quickly she identified a couple of steps she would take in moving towards her goal. Real purpose motivates!

2. **Help them to become 'future focussed'**
   Get them to see the longer-term picture. They only have one life. Where do they see themselves in 5/10 years time?

3. **Help them to see that personal Continuous Improvement is crucial.**
   Doing better today than we did yesterday creates a real positive energy surge for us all. This attitude creates a great and positive atmosphere to work in. How can you support their development.

A final few words:
Not everyone wants the above! Many do however and it's the Leaders responsibility to identify and help these people

Maybe your successor is already there, just waiting for you to help them
Never let it be said of anyone in your Team,
'They died with so much potential!'

Action:

Go and help someone release their potential – for the sake of all concerned

Make reflections on the area covered:

Who needs my help and support today?   What will I do and when?

Month 1	Month 2	Month 3

Actions I must take:

(Where I need to improve..........)

1. _____ by _____ Yes

2. _____ by _____ Yes

3. _____ by _____ Yes

4. _____ by _____ Yes

5. _____ by _____ Yes

6. _____ by _____ Yes

Day 31

The Klein leadership Profile

Welcome to the **KLP**.
It's designed with you in mind – to help you measure your Leadership performance.

It's **your perception** of **your Leadership** values and beliefs.

My experience with Leaders, spanning over thirty years, has enabled me to develop this Profile.

As a Leader you need to be firing in three main areas - the three P's

Purpose and Vision: Effective Leaders know where they are going and know how they are going to get there; they work well in the present and also have a clear picture of the future - where they are heading

People: Effective Leaders have great relationships with those around them. They understand people and know how to get the best out of them.
Followers 'go the extra mile' for those who lead them well

Persistence: Effective Leaders have a great deal of perseverance, even in times of great testing. Performing well in the other two 'P's helps greatly in this area

Now it's time to take the test.

Be honest!!

KLP Questionnaire

Read each statement and mark the degree to which you agree/disagree

		Disagree		Agree		Strongly Agree	
1.	I have a written vision for the next 2/3 years	1	2	3	4	5	6
2.	I regularly communicate my vision to others	1	2	3	4	5	6
3	I have developed a clear plan to achieve my vision	1	2	3	4	5	6
4.	I have developed Specific; Achievable: Measurable goals	1	2	3	4	5	6
5.	I influence people around me	1	2	3	4	5	6
6.	I identify under performance and deal with it	1	2	3	4	5	6
7.	I develop the people around me	1	2	3	4	5	6
8.	I actively coach my staff	1	2	3	4	5	6
9.	I set clear standards across the Team	1	2	3	4	5	6
10.	I encourage others when things are tough	1	2	3	4	5	6
11.	I bounce back when I get setbacks	1	2	3	4	5	6
12.	I am enthusiastic about what I do	1	2	3	4	5	6
13.	I ensure we always complete things	1	2	3	4	5	6
14.	I motivate and support people	1	2	3	4	5	6
15.	I am a good listener	1	2	3	4	5	6
16.	I understand what motivates different people	1	2	3	4	5	6
17.	I challenge people to continually improve their performance	1	2	3	4	5	6
18.	I have developed good relationships at all levels	1	2	3	4	5	6
19.	I have people following me who will 'go the extra mile' for me	1	2	3	4	5	6
20.	I set a clear and good example for others to follow	1	2	3	4	5	6

KLP - Scoring your responses

Question No.	Score	Comments	
1		0 - 10	Serious actions required here
2			
3		11 - 15	Average performance it's time to stretch up!
4			
Total for PURPOSE		16 - 24	Good, but don't get complacent

Question No.	Score	Comments	
5		0 – 24	Why can't you see the real value of people?
6			
7			What areas do you need to improve?
8			
9			
10		25 – 49	Average performance Where can you improve?
11			
12			
13		50 – 59	You're seeing the importance of building good relationships. Time to go for gold
14			
15			How can you do that?
16			
Total for PEOPLE		60 - 72	Excellent Why are you doing so well?

Question No.	Score	Comments	
17		0 - 10	Staying power for any Leader is important
18			What can you do?
19		11 - 15	Average performance Become more consistent!
20			
Total for PERSISTENCE		16 - 24	Good, keep it up and help others

Make reflections on the area covered:

How am I doing with the above?   What will I do and when?

Month 1	Month 2	Month 3

Actions I must take:

(Where I need to improve..........)

1. _____ by _____ Yes

2. _____ by _____ Yes

3. _____ by _____ Yes

4. _____ by _____ Yes

5. _____ by _____ Yes

6. _____ by _____ Yes

Overall Summary

Well done........you've made it and benefitted greatly I hope!!

What now?

Well if this is Month One or Month Two, please do it again. The best way anyone learns is repetition and we Leaders aren't any different.

Also, why not set yourself a target to read a Leadership book over the next four weeks. There are many, many available.

Why not get a colleague or a Team Member to go through this Programme too?

Whatever your reflections or intentions, may I wish you every success as you continue to become a better Leader. Our Teams, Organisations and our Nations need you to.

Acknowledgements:

My thanks to the following who have helped to form and develop my understanding in the vast and always developing area of Leadership.

John Adair	**Three Circle Model of effective Leadership**	Day 7
John Maxwell	**Levels of Leadership**	Day 23
Paul Scanlon **Bradford UK**	**Five 'I's in Individual brilliance**	Day 24